Dear Parents and Educators,

Welcome to Penguin Young Readers! As paren
know that each child develops at his or her own pace—
speech, critical thinking, and, of course, reading. Penguin Young
Readers recognizes this fact. As a result, each Penguin Young Readers
book is assigned a traditional easy-to-read level (1–4) as well as a
Guided Reading Level (A–P). Both of these systems will help you choose
the right book for your child. Please refer to the back of each book
for specific leveling information. Penguin Young Readers features
esteemed authors and illustrators, stories about favorite characters,
fascinating nonfiction, and more!

Welcome, Bao Bao

LEVEL **4**

GUIDED
READING **N**
LEVEL

This book is perfect for a **Fluent Reader** who:
- can read the text quickly with minimal effort;
- has good comprehension skills;
- can self-correct (can recognize when something doesn't sound right); and
- can read aloud smoothly and with expression.

Here are some **activities** you can do during and after reading this book:
- Comprehension: After reading this book, answer the following
  questions.
  - What does *Mei Xiang* mean? What does *Tian Tian* mean?
  - Where were Mei Xiang and Tian Tian born?
  - Why were they brought to the United States?
  - How many giant pandas live in the wild?
  - What does *endangered* mean?
  - What do giant pandas eat?
  - When does a panda cub receive its name?
- Discuss: The United States and China are working together to grow the
  giant panda population. Write a list of actions they have taken, and
  discuss how Mei Xiang, Tian Tian, and Bao Bao are helping.

Remember, sharing the love of reading with a child is the best gift
you can give!

—Bonnie Bader, EdM
  Penguin Young Readers program

To the newest members of our family:
Micah Bernard, Louisa Isabel, and
Samantha Annabelle—GS

PENGUIN YOUNG READERS
Published by the Penguin Group
Penguin Group (USA) LLC, 375 Hudson Street, New York, New York 10014, USA

USA | Canada | UK | Ireland | Australia | New Zealand | India | South Africa | China

penguin.com
A Penguin Random House Company

 Smithsonian

This trademark is owned by the Smithsonian Institution and is registered in the
U.S. Patent and Trademark Office.

Smithsonian Enterprises:
Christopher Liedel, President
Carol LeBlanc, Senior Vice President, Education and Consumer Products
Brigid Ferraro, Vice President, Education and Consumer Products
Ellen Nanney, Licensing Manager
Kealy Gordon, Product Development Manager

Laurie Thompson, Biologist, Giant Panda Habitat
Dr. Brandie Smith, Senior Curator, Giant Panda Habitat
Pamela Baker-Masson, Associate Director of Communications
Jennifer Zoon, Communications Specialist

Photo credits: pages 5, 10, 15, 20, 34, 46, 48 © Tony Yao/Thinkstock; page 11 © C. Q. Young/Thinkstock;
all other photos © National Zoological Park, Smithsonian Institution, courtesy of the following
photographers: Ann Batdorf: pages 6–7, 12; Jessie Cohen: pages 8, 16–17; David Galen: page 45;
Courtney Janney: pages 23, 24, 25; Connor Mallon: page 19; Meghan Murphy: pages 4, 9, 21; Abby
Wood: front cover, title page, 26, 27, 28, 30–33, 35, 37, 38–39, 41, 42–43, 47;
page 14 illustration © Smithsonian's National Zoo.

Library of Congress Cataloging-in-Publication Data is available.

ISBN 978-0-448-48225-5 (pbk)   10 9 8 7 6 5 4 3 2 1
ISBN 978-0-448-48226-2 (hc)   10 9 8 7 6 5 4 3 2 1

PENGUIN YOUNG READERS

LEVEL
FLUENT
READER
4

Smithsonian

WELCOME, BAO BAO

by Gina Shaw

Penguin Young Readers
An Imprint of Penguin Group (USA) LLC

Contents

Meet the Pandas

What are black and white and furry all over? Giant pandas!

Giant pandas belong to the bear family. They have black fur on their ears, around their eyes, and on their **muzzles**.

Mei Xiang

It is on their legs and shoulders, too.
The rest of their coats are white.

Two giant pandas named Mei Xiang
(say: may-SHONG) and Tian Tian (say:
t-YEN t-YEN) live at the Smithsonian's
National Zoo in Washington, DC.

Tian Tian

In the Mandarin Chinese language, Mei Xiang's name means "beautiful fragrance."

When you look at Mei Xiang and Tian Tian, it's hard to tell them apart. But there are some differences between them.

Mei Xiang looks as though she's wearing black "stockings" on her two back legs. The "stockings" reach to the top of her hips. She has black oval patches around her eyes. Mei Xiang weighs about 230 pounds.

Tian Tian looks as though he's wearing black "knee socks." His eye patches are shaped like kidney beans.

Tian Tian is larger than Mei Xiang. He weighs about 260 pounds.

Tian Tian means "more and more" in Mandarin Chinese.

From China to Washington, DC

Mei Xiang and Tian Tian were born in Wolong, Sichuan Province, in China. Giant pandas live in bamboo forests in central China. But people have taken over their **habitat**. There isn't enough space left for the pandas.

There are only about 1,600 giant pandas in the wild. They are an **endangered** species. This means that all giant pandas could die out.

A bamboo forest in China

Many zoos care for giant pandas. Today, there are more than 375 pandas living in zoos around the world.

Zoo workers want to help giant pandas **survive**. They want them to be successful at giving birth to panda cubs. They hope the panda population will grow.

That's why Mei Xiang and Tian Tian came from the China Research and Conservation Center for the Giant Panda in Wolong to the National Zoo in Washington, DC.

At Home with the Pandas

To make Mei Xiang and Tian Tian feel at home, zoo workers set up their exhibit at the National Zoo to look like their natural habitat in China.

The giant pandas can move between indoor and outdoor areas. There are low trees and shrubs that provide shade. Pools and streams help Mei Xiang and Tian Tian cool off on hot days. The giant pandas climb rocks and fallen trees for exercise.

The giant panda outdoor exhibit:
1. Cold water runs through rock caves called grottos. This makes a cool resting place.
2. Trees and bushes create shade.
3. Mist is sprayed to make another cool resting spot.
4. Pools of water are for a dip on hot days.
5. Rocks and tree trunks are for climbing.

Giant pandas keep to themselves in the zoo, just like they do in the wild. They are only brought together when they are going to mate. Mei Xiang and Tian Tian have separate **enclosures**. They do not interact with each other.

But they do interact with food!

What do giant pandas eat? Bamboo, bamboo, and more bamboo!

Giant pandas are mainly **herbivores**. This means they eat mostly plants. In the wild, their diet is made up of 99 percent bamboo. They eat bamboo for 17 hours a day!

At the National Zoo, Mei Xiang and Tian Tian eat bamboo, too. They are fed three times a day. Their largest feeding is in the evening. They are each given 40 pounds of bamboo just to get them through the night!

Tian Tian munches on bamboo.

Because giant pandas eat so much bamboo, zoo workers grow their own supply of this plant. They also give Mei Xiang and Tian Tian apples, carrots, sweet potatoes, pears, and biscuits that are made for animals that eat plants. This food **supplements** their diets and is used as rewards during training.

Tian Tian eats a fruit snack in the afternoon. Yum!

Something New at the Zoo

On August 23, 2013, something very exciting happened at the National Zoo. A baby panda was born to Mei Xiang and Tian Tian. It was a girl!

The zookeepers and **veterinarians**, known as the panda team, watched Mei Xiang give birth to her cub. A panda cam had been set up in the giant panda exhibit. The panda team watched Mei Xiang pick up the cub, cradle her in her arms, and lick her as soon as she was born. They could hear the sounds the cub was making, too.

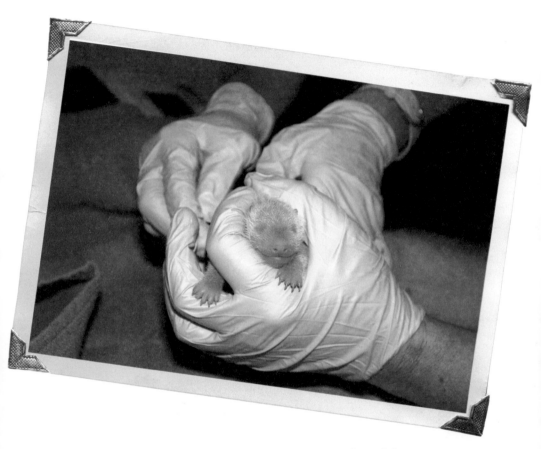

According to Chinese custom, the panda cub will be given a name when she is 100 days old.

Cub Care

Two days later, the veterinarians gave the panda cub her first **examination**. The cub was fully formed. She was a bright, healthy shade of pink. She weighed 4.8 ounces (137 grams). Her heartbeat was steady.

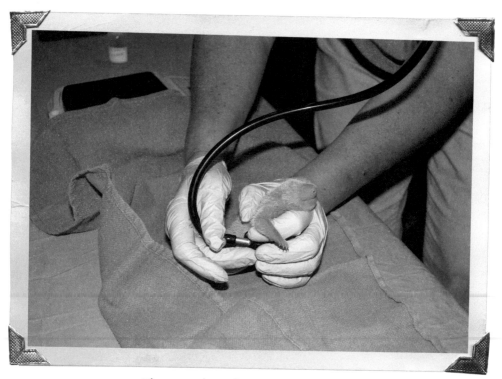

The panda cub on August 25, 2013

The panda cub on September 3, 2013

The zoo doctors were able to hear her breathing. Her belly was full, and her mouth was normal. This meant the cub was nursing and digesting her mother's milk. The panda team was happy to see that the cub was healthy.

The panda cub was examined
regularly over the next months.
She had her ears checked.

She was weighed.

The vets listened to her heart
and took her temperature.

They measured her.

As the cub gets older, zookeepers see that her eye markings are shaped like Mei Xiang's. But the markings on her back are like Tian Tian's.

Tian Tian is very easygoing. He is **motivated** by food and is easy to train. But he will only do activities that are simple for him. If something is too hard, he just won't do it.

Mei Xiang is very careful about everything she does. She is a bit nervous, too. She doesn't like loud noises and will react to them.

The panda cub is easygoing, just like her dad. Most of the time, she is relaxed when she is handled by the panda team. But sometimes she has had enough!

When the panda cub was almost two months old, the veterinarians examined her again. Since her first health check, the cub had more than doubled her weight. She now weighed a little less than two pounds and had the black markings

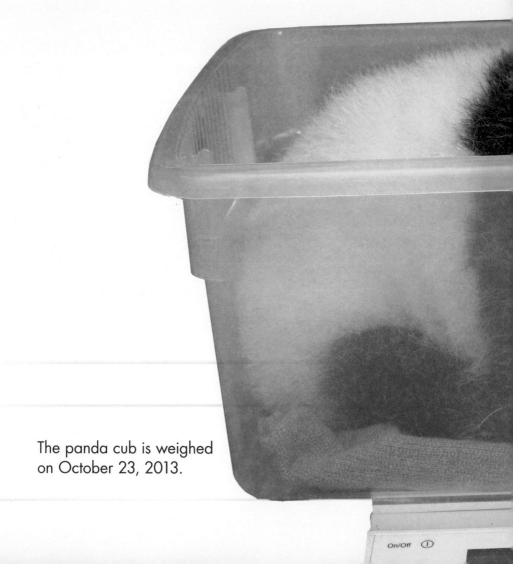

The panda cub is weighed on October 23, 2013.

On/Off ○

of a giant panda. Her eyes were not opened yet. A panda cub's eyes don't open until about 40 to 60 days after it's born.

The panda team thinks that Mei Xiang is a very loving mother to her cub. She feeds her, grooms her, cradles her, and watches her very carefully.

Tian Tian is never alone with the cub. He doesn't have anything to do with raising her. It could be dangerous to the cub to put them together. In the wild, only panda mothers take care of their cubs. The fathers never meet their cubs.

The Naming Ceremony

The 100th day of the panda cub's life is here!

When the cub was born, the National Zoo asked several important people to come up with Mandarin Chinese names for the baby panda. Then they asked people around the world to vote on the name on the National Zoo's website.

Here are the five names that voters could choose from:

Bao Bao (宝宝) (say: bow-BOW)—precious treasure

Ling Hua (玲花) (say: ling-HWA)—darling, delicate flower

Long Yun (龙韵) (say: long-YOON)— *long* is the Chinese symbol of the dragon, and *yun* means charming. When put together, this is a sign of luck for panda cooperation between China and the United States.

Mulan (木兰) (say: moo-LAHN)— a smart and brave Chinese warrior from the fifth century; it also means magnolia flower in Chinese.

Zhen Bao (珍宝) (say: jen-BAO)— treasure, valuable

On December 1, 2013, after 100 days and 123,039 votes, the giant panda cub receives her name: Bao Bao!

The naming ceremony included special video messages from the First Lady of the United States, Michelle Obama, and the First Lady of the People's Republic of China, Peng Liyuan.

At the end of the ceremony, Chinese lion dancers led guests to the giant panda exhibit. Tian Tian even received a frozen treat.

On January 6, 2014, the zookeepers felt Bao Bao was ready to meet the press. She made headlines!

The giant panda exhibit was opened to visitors on January 18, 2014. Now everybody could welcome Bao Bao!

Bao Bao Goes Out

At first, Bao Bao stayed with Mei Xiang in the inside area of the giant panda exhibit. She learned to walk and then to climb on the rock walls. She played with her ball and her other toys.

After playing all morning, Bao Bao falls into a deep sleep. She naps for several hours at a time.

Bao Bao climbs on a rock wall inside Mei Xiang's enclosure. The zookeepers have "baby-proofed" the area by putting hay behind the rock in case Bao Bao falls.

On April 1, 2014, Bao Bao went outside for the first time. The zookeepers said she was a little nervous at first. But Mei Xiang reassured her cub. So Bao Bao went into the outdoor yard. She began to explore and even climbed on a small tree. But she never strayed too far from Mei Xiang's side.

Growing Up

Bao Bao grew strong teeth. She still fed on her mother's milk. But she was introduced to bamboo shoots, too. She was also given treats such as watered-down apple juice and cooked sweet potatoes. These will be used as training rewards as Bao Bao gets older.

As a young cub, Bao Bao's daily routine was simple: sleeping, playing, and growing!

At about 18 months old, Bao Bao stopped nursing. She was slowly separated from Mei Xiang until she was ready for her own enclosure at the zoo.

Bao Bao celebrates her first birthday with a cake made of frozen fruit juice and treats.

Bao Bao will be sent to China when she turns four to go into the breeding program there. She will be able to have her own cubs when she is between five and seven years old. She is doing her part, along with Mei Xiang, Tian Tian, and the zookeepers and scientists, to help keep the world's panda population growing!

Until then, Bao Bao's always at home . . . at the National Zoo!

Millions of people come to see Bao Bao every year.

Glossary

enclosure: an area that is surrounded by a wall or a fence

endangered: a living thing that could die out and become extinct

examination: the act of looking at something closely and carefully

habitat: a place or environment where an animal normally lives

herbivore: an animal that eats plants

motivate: to give a reason for doing something

muzzle: an animal's nose, mouth, and jaws

supplement: something that supplies what is needed or makes an addition

survive: to continue to live

veterinarian: a doctor who takes care of animals